Spotlight on the
MAYA, AZTEC, and INCA CIVILIZATIONS

Ancient AZTEC GEOGRAPHY

Barbara M. Linde

PowerKiDS
press™

NEW YORK

Published in 2017 by The Rosen Publishing Group, Inc.
29 East 21st Street, New York, NY 10010

Editor: Katie Kawa
Book Design: Tanya Dellaccio

Photo Credits: Cover, pp. 5, 13 DEA/G. DAGLI ORTI/Getty Images; p. 4 https://commons.wikimedia.org/wiki/File:Flag_of_Mexico.svg; p. 7 https://commons.wikimedia.org/wiki/File:Map_of_Tenochtitlan,_1524.jpg; p. 8 Julio Aldana/Shutterstock.com; p. 9 Leon Rafael/Shutterstock.com; p. 10 https://commons.wikimedia.org/wiki/File:Murales_Rivera_-_Markt_in_Tlatelolco_3.jpg; pp. 11, 26 https://commons.wikimedia.org/wiki/File:Reconstruction_of_Tenochtitlan2006.jpg; p. 15 https://commons.wikimedia.org/wiki/File:Acueducto_de_Chapultepec,_parte_posterior.jpg; p. 16 https://commons.wikimedia.org/wiki/File:Jaguar_warrior.jpg; p. 17 https://commons.wikimedia.org/wiki/File:Montezuma_from_An_Illustrated_History_of_the_New_World.jpg; p. 19 National Geographic/Getty Images; p. 21 (top) https://commons.wikimedia.org/wiki/File:Pochtecas_con_su_carga.JPG; pp. 21 (bottom), 27 Werner Forman/Getty Images; p. 22 Valentyn Volkov/Shutterstock.com; p. 23 (both) https://commons.wikimedia.org/wiki/File:The_Florentine_Codex-_Agriculture.tiff; p. 25 David Hiser/Getty Images; p. 29 Dan Kitwood/Getty Images.

Library of Congress Cataloging-in-Publication Data

Names: Linde, Barbara M.
Title: Ancient Aztec geography / Barbara M. Linde.
Description: New York : PowerKids Press, 2017. | Series: Spotlight on the Maya, Aztec, and Inca civilizations | Includes index.
Identifiers: ISBN 9781499419092 (pbk.) | ISBN 9781499419122 (library bound) | ISBN 9781499419108 (6 pack)
Subjects: LCSH: Aztecs--Juvenile literature. | Aztecs--Civilization--Juvenile literature. | Indians of Mexico--History--Juvenile literature.
Classification: LCC F1219.73 L56 2017 | DDC 972'.018--dc23

CPSIA Compliance Information: Batch #BS16PK For further information contact Rosen Publishing, New York, New York at 1-800-237-9932.

CONTENTS

THE NOMADS

Before the Aztec people established a powerful empire, they were **nomads**. Historians believe they came from what's now northern Mexico. Aztec legends call their original homeland Aztlán. They began traveling south and eventually reached the lands that became part of the Aztec Empire in what's now central and southern Mexico.

According to legend, these nomads believed their sun and war god, Huitzilopochtli, would help them find a permanent home. They believed the god told them to look for an eagle sitting on a cactus. The eagle would be eating a serpent, or snake. Aztec legend states that the wanderers finally saw this sign around 1325, when the cactus, eagle, and serpent were spotted on an island in the middle of Lake Texcoco. The nomads finally found a home. The Aztec people would be influenced by the geography of this location for centuries.

MEXICAN FLAG

The Mexican flag includes an eagle sitting on a cactus and eating a serpent. This is meant to honor the Aztec people who once called the lands of Mexico home.

THE VALLEY OF MEXICO

The Aztecs first settled in the Valley of Mexico. This valley is a plateau that rises high above sea level in what's now central Mexico. A plateau is a large, flat area of land. It can be enclosed by mountains, which is true of the Valley of Mexico.

The Valley of Mexico is also a basin where water pools instead of draining into a river or stream. During the time of the Aztec people, this region's water was found mainly in lakes. Lake Texcoco was the largest of five lakes in the Valley of Mexico while the Aztec people were in power.

A mountain range called the Sierra Madre Occidental is on the western side of the Valley of Mexico. The Sierra Madre Oriental is the range on the eastern side. The Sierra Madre del Sur range is to the south. Active volcanoes were also found in the Valley of Mexico. These landforms shaped not only the geography of this region, but also the lives of the Aztec people who lived there.

Shown here is a map of the Aztec capital city, which was located where the Aztec people first settled. The Aztec civilization grew from a small island settlement in Lake Texcoco into an empire that stretched across large parts of today's Mexico.

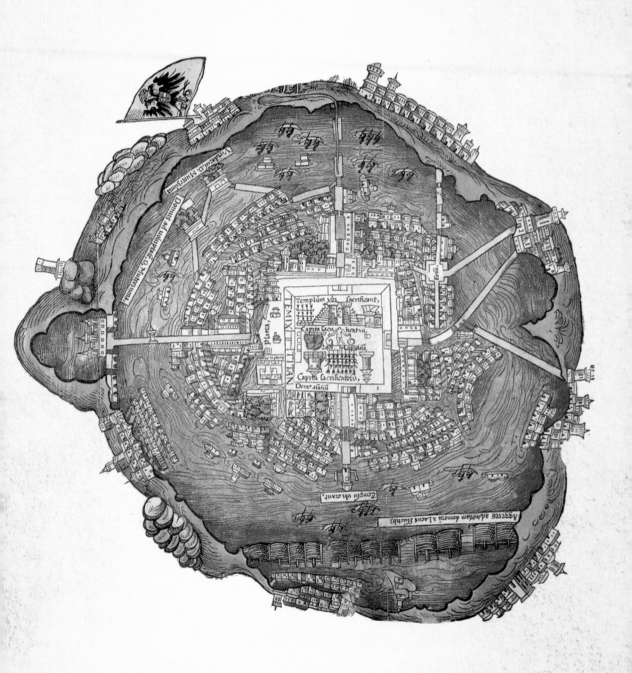

GEOGRAPHY AND CLIMATE

Geography and climate are strongly connected. Different parts of the Aztec Empire dealt with different kinds of weather because of their geographic location and landforms. Temperatures in the Valley of Mexico ranged from very hot during the day in the summer to very cold on winter nights. Because of this area's height above sea level, it wasn't unusual for frost and snow to occur at certain times of the year. However, an early frost could destroy crops for Aztec farmers.

TLALOC

The Aztec people depended on agriculture for survival, and a good harvest depended on the weather. That's why Tlaloc was an important Aztec god.

This statue, which is believed to represent Tlaloc, stands outside the National Museum of Anthropology in Mexico City.

The rainy season in the lands of the Aztec Empire generally lasted from May through September or October. The most rain fell in the coastal regions of the empire.

The Aztecs believed a god named Tlaloc controlled the rain. He could send rain to crops, or he could keep the rain away and create a drought. Droughts were scary for the people because without water, the crops died and there was no food.

BUILDING A CITY

Settling on an island was a wise move for the Aztecs. Geography worked in their favor. Lake Texcoco was large. Mountains surrounded it. This meant that enemies would have a hard time getting to the island to harm the Aztec people.

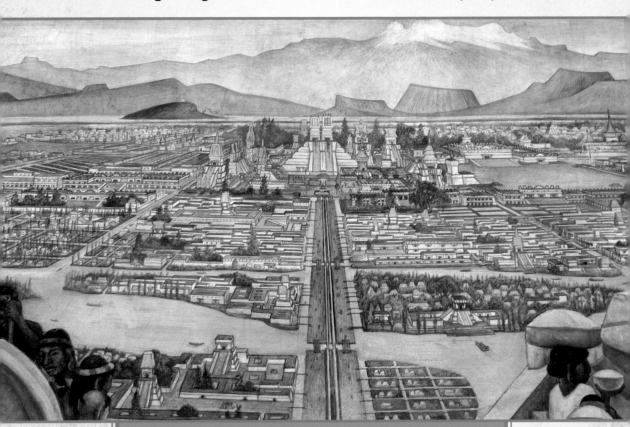

Because of the geography of Tenochtitlán, people often had to travel to, from, and around the city by canoe. The canals that ran through Tenochtitlán were an important part of the city's design.

The Aztec people went to work building a city on this island. They designed and laid it out carefully. To make the island larger and sturdier, workers **fortified** some of the shallow swampland with mud from the lake and the shore. The streets and many canals formed a **grid**. Three raised roads called causeways connected the center of this island city to the mainland. Each causeway had bridges that could be moved to let canoes go through or keep unwanted visitors out.

The Aztec people called this city Tenochtitlán. It became the capital of the Aztec Empire.

THE LAYOUT OF TENOCHTITLÁN

A large wall enclosed the center of Tenochtitlán, which was called the Sacred Precinct. Historians believe this section of the city was more than 300,000 square feet (27,870.9 sq m) in area. Gates connected the Sacred Precinct to the city's causeways.

The capital's main temple, smaller temples, and other places of religious importance—including a ball court—were found inside the Sacred Precinct. Just outside the precinct walls were palaces, a large marketplace, and government buildings. The smaller houses of the common people were located in the outer parts of the city. These homes were often made of reeds and mud.

Tenochtitlán grew to more than 5 square miles (13 sq km) in size. More than 140,000 people lived there at the height of the Aztec Empire. It was one of the largest cities in the world.

Archaeologists are still finding ruins at the former site of Tenochtitlán. These ruins help us learn more about how this island city grew and what it looked like. Shown here are ruins from the city's main temple.

TECHNOLOGY IN THE CAPITAL

The geography of Tenochtitlán strongly influenced the way **technology** developed in this city. Lake Texcoco's water was salty, so the people of Tenochtitlán needed another source for fresh drinking water. Clever Aztec engineers built an **aqueduct** to bring freshwater from mainland springs to the city.

Aztec engineers used the causeway that ran from a part of the empire called Chapultepec as a base for the aqueduct. This aqueduct was 3 miles (4.8 km) long. As Tenochtitlán grew in population and power, more clean water was needed. This led to the construction of another aqueduct.

Lake Texcoco sometimes flooded during the rainy season. To protect the city, engineers built a dike that kept the water out. A dike is a wall or mound of earth used to keep out water and prevent floods. Aqueducts and dikes are examples of ways the Aztec people overcame challenges presented by the land and water around them.

The Chapultepec aqueduct was replaced by the Spanish during the time they ruled Mexico. Part of that aqueduct is shown here.

THE GROWTH OF THE EMPIRE

Aztec leaders used different methods to expand their empire into new lands. Their children sometimes married into the ruling families of nearby cities to form alliances. Wars also helped the Aztec Empire grow. Its strong, fierce warriors conquered other groups. This allowed the Aztec Empire to spread over more parts of what's now Mexico. After many years, the empire reached from the Gulf of Mexico to the Pacific Ocean.

The Aztec Empire was divided into city-states, or self-governing areas made up of a city and the surrounding lands. Each city-state had its own leader. The Aztec emperor was the leader of the capital city of Tenochtitlán.

AZTEC WARRIOR

All the city-states under Aztec rule had to offer tribute to the emperor. This was payment in the form of crops and other goods, warriors, or slaves. People traveled throughout the empire to collect tribute and bring it back to Tenochtitlán.

MONTEZUMA II

The Aztec Empire was made up of many different groups of people from different parts of what we now call Mexico. Every conquered city-state had to pay tribute to the emperor. Shown here is Montezuma II, who was the Aztec emperor when the Spanish arrived in Aztec lands in 1519.

OTHER AZTEC SETTLEMENTS

Every city in the Aztec Empire was carefully planned. Major Aztec cities had temples, palaces where the leaders lived, and a marketplace. The city of Tlatelolco was known for its marketplace, which was the largest in the Aztec Empire. Tlatelolco was located on the same island as Tenochtitlán. These two cities were sometimes called sister cities, and they merged, or combined, to form one city during the height of the Aztec Empire.

Other Aztec cities and villages were much smaller than Tlatelolco and Tenochtitlán. Capilco and Cuexcomate were located south of Tenochtitlán. Archaeologists have studied ruins found where these settlements once stood. They believe Capilco had about 21 houses, while Cuexcomate had about 150. Yautepec, which was also located south of Tenochtitlán, was larger. It was the capital of a city-state. Artifacts found where these cities and villages once stood help us learn about the different places where Aztec people lived.

Shown here is an illustration of what historians believe the Tlatelolco marketplace looked like. It was a busy part of the Aztec Empire!

TRADE AND TRAVEL

The Aztec people developed a system of roads to connect the lands of their empire. Runners delivered messages between cities. The roads also helped trade in the growing empire.

Trade was an important part of the Aztec economy. Trading allowed people to get food and other goods from different parts of the empire and even from beyond the empire's borders.

The *pochteca*, or traveling Aztec merchants, journeyed along trade routes throughout the empire and into foreign lands. Often gone for months, they returned with food and other goods for sale. They also brought items for the rich **nobles**, such as feathers and gems. This work wasn't easy because the *pochteca* traveled on foot for many miles each day. They traveled through mountain ranges and deserts. As the empire expanded, they even traveled into rain forest regions to trade. Many of the feathers these merchants brought back came from birds that lived in the rain forests.

Marketplaces, such as the one recreated in this image, were locations where goods from different geographic regions could be bought and sold. The *pochteca* were responsible for traveling to these regions to bring back **exotic** goods, as well as more familiar local goods.

POCHTECA

WORKING WITH THE LAND

Farming was the main job in the Aztec Empire. Aztec farmers found ways to work with the land around them in order to produce enough crops to keep the empire fed. The Aztec people used simple hand tools for planting, weeding, and harvesting. They didn't have large animals or wheels to help them farm.

The Aztec people grew maize (corn), squash, beans, tomatoes, avocados, and chili peppers for food. They grew cotton plants and maguey plants for fibers to make clothes.

As the Aztec Empire expanded, new crops were introduced to the Aztec people. Cacao was one such crop. Cacao beans, which are also called cocoa beans, were used as a kind of currency, or money, and in a chocolate drink for Aztec nobles. They were offered as tribute from conquered people living near rain forests.

Aztec farmers found ways to grow crops in places that weren't fit for traditional farming methods. In areas of the empire with many hills or mountains, farmers built flat steps into the slopes for space to grow crops. This is called terrace farming. **Irrigation** was also used throughout the empire. Farmers directed saved rainwater or water from rivers and streams to their crops.

Tenochtitlán and other cities built on lakes didn't have enough solid land on which to grow crops, so Aztec farmers had to find a way to make geography work for them. In this case, they used the lakes and marshes around them as another location for farming. The Aztec people made islands for growing crops. These islands are known as chinampas. Tall wooden poles anchored the chinampas to the lakebed. To make fertile soil, farmers used mud from the lake bottom layered with rotting plants.

The rectangular chinampas covered much of the lake near Tenochtitlán. Farmers in canoes used the canals between the chinampas to travel around these island gardens. They could then pick the ripe crops and deliver the crops to the markets. Chinampas proved to be a successful way to grow crops in an environment that wasn't **typically** used as farmland.

Chinampas were so successful that farmers in Mexico still use them today.

THE IMPORTANCE OF WATER

Water was an important natural resource in the Aztec Empire. People paddled their canoes in the canals to get around parts of the empire. Water was needed to grow crops. The water protected the island city of Tenochtitlán from invasion. **Artisans** mixed clay with water to make bowls, jugs, and other types of pottery.

Mud from Lake Texcoco was also a useful natural resource. This mud helped create and expand Tenochtitlán. The Aztecs used mud to make the chinampas they needed for farming. Houses were built with sun-dried mud bricks.

Tenochtitlán, shown in this illustration, was surrounded by water. Water was used by the Aztec people for transportation, farming, drinking, and many other important purposes.

Some of the canals used for traveling around the Aztec Empire can still be seen in a part of Mexico called Xochimilco, shown here.

Tall, strong plants called reeds grew up from the bottom of lakes. Farmers used these reeds to make chinampas. The reeds made excellent roofs for houses. Palm trees, cacti, and aloe plants also grew around bodies of water. Weavers used fibers from these plants to make baskets, mats, and other goods used in Aztec homes.

MORE NATURAL RESOURCES

The Aztec Empire was rich in natural resources. The Valley of Mexico was home to many wild animals hunted by the Aztec people for food, including deer, gophers, armadillos, and other small animals. They also hunted rabbits, jaguars, and **ocelots** for their skins. The lakes and rivers of this region were full of fish, **waterfowl**, and insects for the Aztec people to eat.

Obsidian is a hard volcanic glass found in lands that were part of the Aztec Empire. It was used to make tools and weapons. Metals were also found throughout the lands of the empire. These included copper, lead, silver, and tin. As the empire expanded, gold also became an important metal to the Aztec people. Metals and stones were often used to make jewelry and statues.

The Aztec people used trees to make canoes. Wood was also used to make certain statues and masks for religious ceremonies.

This Aztec mask is made of wood and covered with valuable stones, including a blue-green stone called turquoise. The Aztecs acquired turquoise from places north of the empire's borders, including areas that are now part of the American Southwest.

REMINDERS OF THE PAST

In 1519, Hernán Cortés led a group of Spanish forces into Aztec territory. His goal was to conquer the Aztec people and use their natural resources—especially their gold—to make Spain wealthier. In 1521, Cortés and his men captured Tenochtitlán. The powerful Aztec Empire fell to the Spanish.

Today, Mexico City is the capital of Mexico, but an ancient city lies mostly buried underneath it. That ancient city is Tenochtitlán. People are excavating, or digging up, some of the ruins of Tenochtitlán that can be found under Mexico City. They hope these ruins will reveal more about the Aztec Empire.

From the writings and artifacts left behind, we already know the Aztec people worked with the land and resources around them not just to survive but to **thrive**. As archaeologists discover more artifacts and ruins, they hope to learn even more about the Aztec people and the land they called home.

GLOSSARY

aqueduct (AH-kwuh-duhkt): A man-made channel constructed to move water from one place to another.

artisan (AAR-tuh-zuhn): A skilled worker who makes things with their hands.

exotic (ihg-ZAH-tihk): From another country or place; out of the ordinary.

fortify (FOR-tuh-fy): To add material for strengthening or improving.

grid (GRIHD): A network of lines that cross each other to make equal-sized squares.

irrigation (eer-uh-GAY-shun): The supplying of water to land by man-made means.

noble (NOH-buhl): A person who belongs to a high social class.

nomad (NOH-mad): A person who has no fixed home but wanders from place to place.

ocelot (AH-suh-laht): A wildcat that lives in the Americas and has a yellow or gray coat with black markings.

technology (tehk-NAH-luh-jee): The way people do something and the tools they use.

thrive (THRYV): To grow successfully.

typically (TIH-pih-klee): Generally or normally.

waterfowl (WAA-tuhr-foul): A bird that lives in or near water.

INDEX

PRIMARY SOURCE LIST

Page 7: Map of Tenochtitlán. Colorized woodcut based on the original by Hernán Cortés and printed in Nuremberg, Germany. 1524. Original kept at the Newberry Library, Chicago, Illinois.

Page 21 (top): Image from the Florentine Codex. Compiled by Fray Bernardino de Sahagún. ca. 1529–1588. Now kept at the Laurentian Library, Florence, Italy.

Page 23 (both): Page from the Florentine Codex. Compiled by Fray Bernardino de Sahagún. ca. 1529–1588. Now kept at the Laurentian Library, Florence, Italy.

Page 29: Turquoise mosaic mask. Creator unknown. ca. 1400–1521. Cedro wood covered with turquoise, mother-of-pearl, conch shell, and cinnabar. Now kept at the British Museum, London, UK.

WEBSITES

Due to the changing nature of Internet links, PowerKids Press has developed an online list of websites related to the subject of this book. This site is updated regularly. Please use this link to access the list: www.powerkidslinks.com/soac/azgeo